Killer Puzzles

Find the Phantom of Ghastly Castle

Kjartan Poskitt

Illustrated by Steve Cox

Hippo

Scholastic Children's Books,
Commonwealth House, 1-19 New Oxford Street
London WC1A 1NU, UK

A division of Scholastic Ltd
London ~ New York ~ Toronto ~ Sydney ~ Auckland

First published in the UK by Scholastic Ltd, 1994
This edition published 1996

Text copyright © Kjartan Poskitt, 1994
Inside illustrations copyright © Steve Cox, 1994
Cover illustration copyright © Chris Fisher, 1996

ISBN 0 590 13660 7

Dear Reader,

Ghastly Castle was built on top of Carcass Crag just outside the village of Much Wailing. In daytime you can see giant rooks flying around the castle turrets. At night, fiendish laughter rings from the windows. Worst of all there is a terrible Phantom trapped inside the castle!

This is the book of Ghastly Castle, and the Phantom is trapped between these pages! Your task is to find it. Maybe you're scared already? Never mind, then. Just pass this book to a tough friend and forget it. Go and watch telly or clean your room or something. But maybe you want to see the Phantom? Do you? You'll have to be brilliantly brave and completely cool.... and of course, intensely intelligent! Think you are? Well, then I DARE you to study this book very carefully because in the end, with your very own eyes you might just see....

The Phantom of Ghastly Castle!

The Story of the Phantom

Many years ago there was just a small wooden hovel on top of Carcass Crag, where a strange old woman lived. When Sir Gustave Ghastly decided to build his castle there, she refused to move unless Sir Gustave offered her a room in his castle.

Sir Gustave had an odd feeling about the old woman, and in the end he agreed to her demands. However, as soon as she had stepped inside the room, Sir Gustave had it sealed up for ever.

Now, hundreds of years later, the Phantom of the old woman still haunts the same room. So, if you can find which room is sealed up . . .

YOU MIGHT SEE THE PHANTOM

How to find the Sealed Room

Using this book as a guide, your task is to go round the Castle visiting every room you can.

There's an index of all the rooms on pages 94 and 95 of this book, where you should keep track of where you've been and what you've found.

1. Start at the Gate House, which is the way into the Castle (page 8). Solve the puzzle to find the next place you can visit, and then look through the book to find it.

2. Keep moving from room to room as indicated by the puzzles and signs. Solve the puzzles as you go.

3. In some rooms you might find a *useful item* such as a key or a magic number to help you as you go exploring. You'll need the useful items to get through some rooms. Keep track of them in the index at the back of the book.

4. You MUST follow the instructions to reach each room in turn as if you were actually walking round the Castle and complete each puzzle before you move on. If you cheat, you will NEVER find the Phantom!

Turn the page for some hints!

Hints

Where do doors lead?

1. Some doors in the Castle don't have obvious signs, but you will find other clues to tell you where they lead.

2. All doors and secret panels are unlocked and you can go through them ... unless you are given different instructions. Once a door is unlocked, then it stays open.

3. Important: Some doors *cannot* be reached or opened. Obviously this means that you *must not* go through them!

Which way to go?

Some rooms lead to more than one place. Try them all. If you reach a dead end, then you'll have to double back.

Useful items

To get through some rooms, you might need a useful item. For instance, if you look at the instructions for the Catacombs (on page 40) you'll see that you can't get through unless you've already gone to get the CANDLE which is in another room. If you try to go through without the CANDLE, you could be lost in this book for ever!

Evil laughs

Every time you solve a puzzle, it's a good idea to do your
very own *evil laugh*. Try and do an evil laugh now. Go on . . .
Har har har har!

A map

It's a good idea to get a pencil and a big piece of paper to
make a map as you go along. You can mark all the rooms
and doors and secret passages on it. That way, if you get
stuck you can find your way out again.

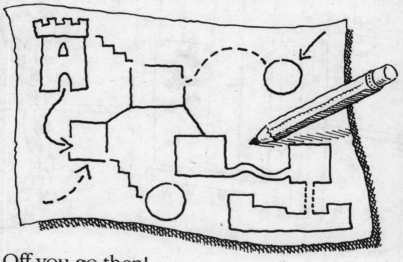

Off you go then!

Explore as much as you possibly can. Eventually you will
find there is only one room you can't visit, and if you're *very*
observant you will have found instructions on how to see
the Phantom! Do a massive evil laugh and then turn to the
haunted room . . . good luck!

The Gate House

The only way into the Castle is up the mountain path and across the drawbridge, which leads you into the Gate House.

Chained to the wall is the GATE KEY which will only undo one of the locks. Can you tell which gate you can unlock and go through?

To find out where the open gate leads to, look through the book to find the other side of the gate with the same pattern!

The Dungeon

This is the Dungeon, and when the Castle was built there was only one way into it from a hidden door somewhere else in the Castle.

When Sir Gustave caught four gnomes fishing in his moat, he sent them down here for life. It seemed a bit unfair, because life for gnomes can be a *very* long time! Despite the fact that the door was never locked, they have each started an escape route.

In fact, the only gnome who has finished is 173 years old.
    If you can work out which is the finished route, you can
use it . . . if you dare!

The Marble Passage

The Marble Passage is guarded by a very fierce beast! It's so fierce that we daren't show you what it looks like, but if you're brave enough to find out then join the dots . . .

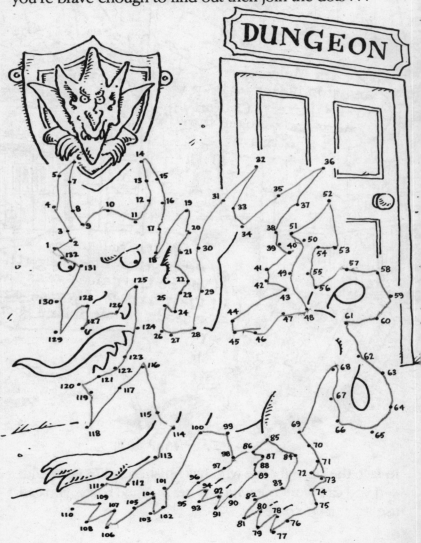

It's *so* scary that the only thing that will frighten it away is its own reflection, so don't even think of stepping into the passage unless you have the MIRROR!

By the way, you'll see that the beast's tail is pointing at one of the doors. It is a *false* door and doesn't go anywhere!

The Great Hall

When you enter the Great Hall you will see that the floor is made up of huge stones in five different patterns. The stones are so big that you can't jump across any of them; you have to step from one to another in turn.

Just to be awkward, Sir Gustave made a rule! When you arrive in a doorway, you can choose two of the different patterns. You must then cross the hall *only stepping on the two patterns you have chosen.*

If you step on more than two patterns, the suit of armour will fire its axe at you. It's not really worth risking, is it?

(You can choose a different pair of patterns each time you arrive at the Hall.)

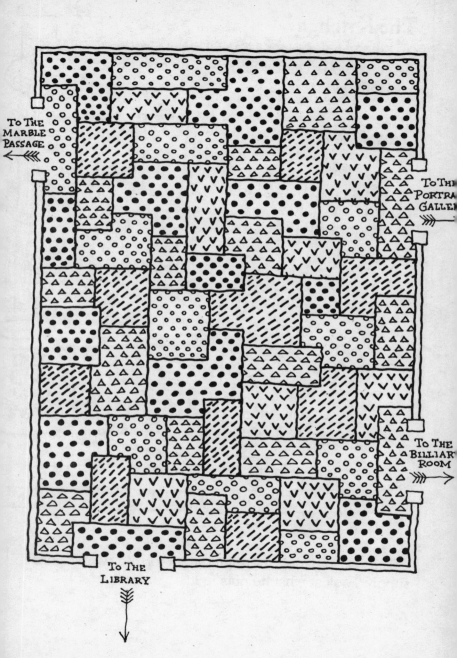

TO THE
MARBLE
PASSAGE

TO THE
PORTRAIT
GALLERY

TO THE
BILLIARD
ROOM

TO THE
LIBRARY

The Kitchen

On the Kitchen table is a CANDLE, but Gristle the cook won't let you borrow it unless you help him out.

Gristle is preparing the ingredients for the winter gravy supply. Look at what he puts in it!

He only has some balance scales and four weights of 1kg, 3kg, 20kg and 27kg. Can you show Gristle how to arrange the weights on the scales so he can weigh out exactly 9 kg of bat's liver?

The Belfry

This is the Belfry, where the bell-ringers used to ring the bells by pulling on the bell ropes. One bellringer must have swung right through the wall into the next room!

The number on each bell is how much the bell weighs in tonnes!

If you pull on the three ropes hanging in the middle, what is the total weight in tonnes of the bells that would ring? This is a MAGIC NUMBER!

"The Bells! The Bells! AND OTHER BELFRY HITS

The Nursery

This is the Nursery. Children would scream all night to be let out of here, because some nasty creatures used to come out of the hole under the rug in the middle of the night and prod the bed with sharp sticks!

But where does the hole in the floor lead to? The building blocks have the clue.

Using each block once, form a row of matching letters to spell out what is down the hole.

The Games Room

In the Games Room, all the floor tiles are playing-cards!

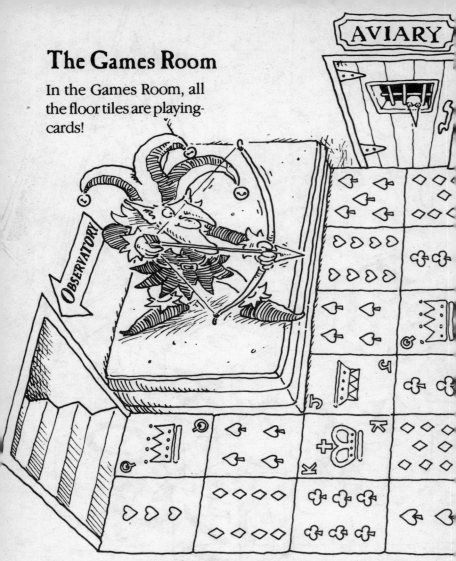

But beware, Sir Gustave liked *horrid* games and the floor is booby-trapped!

To get from one door to another, step across one tile at a time. You can move up, down, across or diagonally.

Add up the points on the cards as you go, because you must reach another door in thirty-five points or less!

If you go over thirty-five points, or if you step on any of the picture cards, the joker will shoot a deadly dart at you!

The Library

You can tell someone's been doing a lot of work in here. Just look at all the books lying about!

There is one obvious door which is unlocked and goes through to the Great Hall. However if you pull the bookcase out, behind it you'll find a second door! This door won't open, but to find out more about it put the books in position on the shelves!

When you've put all the books in the right place, read the message spelt out by the letters on the backs of the books.

The Turret

The Turret is guarded by a FOWEL BYRDE!

YE CHART FOR SCARING AWAY FOWEL BYRDES

1 Blunderbuss

2 Net

3 Scarecrow

4 Rook Poison

BYRDE SEEDE WITH BONES

Join the dots to see which of Sir Gustave's flying mutants is blocking your path. Then consult the chart to find out which item you need to frighten it out of your way.

The Battlements

The Battlements are divided into two sections. The Lower Battlements are reached by some steps and lead to two doors.

The Upper Battlements lead to one door and more steps. The Battlements are separated by an old rusty gate. You'll need the HACKSAW to get it open.

Unfortunately, some naughty, evil person has scrambled up all the letters on the signs. Can you work out what each sign should say?

The Portrait Gallery

In the Portrait Gallery there are two staircases and two doors you can go through. There is also one door which is permanently nailed up.

Above the doors is a row of six pictures. When they were hung up the artist had strict instructions:

Lady Skullkiss was not to be at the end. Lord and Lady Grimchops were to be next to each other. The Duchess of Redgore was next but one to Baron Bloodclot, who refused to be next to Lord Grimchops. Sir Gustave Ghastly was next to one of the women.

Can you work out which is Sir Gustave's portrait?

You'll see that each portrait is numbered. The number below Sir Gustave's portrait is a MAGIC NUMBER!

The Armoury

This is where Sir Gustave's craftsmen used to mend all his fighting equipment, so it's a good place to find some useful tools.

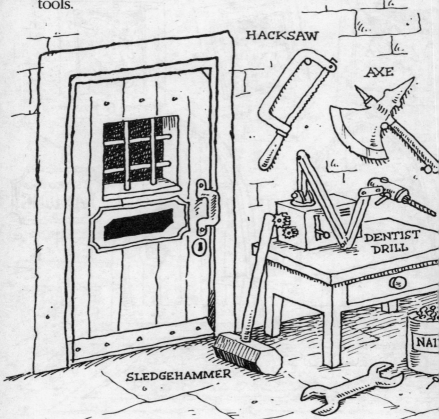

It's also a good place to find a secret door! One of the shields will swing open to reveal a hole in the wall. If you climb through the hole you'll find some steps which go down to a mystery door. Can you tell which shield it is?

The mystery door leads into another room, but you'll never know which one . . . unless you've found the secret message elsewhere in the castle!

The Wine Cellar

Gosh it's dusty in here! In fact it's so dusty that you'll have to have a drink before you move on.

Unfortunately, all these bottles are empty.

Each of these drinks is a mixture from two of the bottles. Can you unscramble the letters and see if you can find a safe drink . . .

PANTRY

but it might not taste very nice!

The Pink Bedroom

The Pink Bedroom is totally gross!

It has been taken over by YE SLYMIE SNAYLES. Yuk!

Their slime trails are so sticky that you mustn't risk stepping over them, or you might get stuck for *ever*!
Can you find a way across the room?

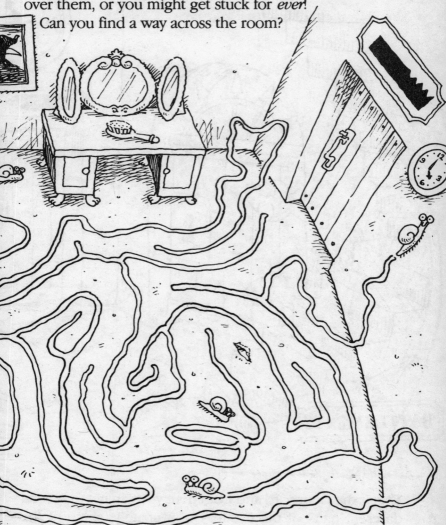

(And you're not allowed to walk up the walls, either!)

The Courtyard

BATTLEMENTS

This is the Courtyard and from here you can get to several different parts of the Castle. Unfortunately, some of the signs showing where you can go are broken, but you might find the missing pieces later.

There's only one door here that you *can't* go through, because it's bricked up on the other side.

Look at the Castle clock. In about 217 minutes, both hands will be pointing at the bricked-up door.

Can you tell which door it is?

The Catacombs

BEWARE! These are the tunnels where all Sir Gustave Ghastly's dead relatives have been laid to rest! It is *very* dark and so to get through you must have the CANDLE!

Be very careful walking through the Catacombs, because if you step over any bones a Ghastly Ghoul will appear and gobble you up.

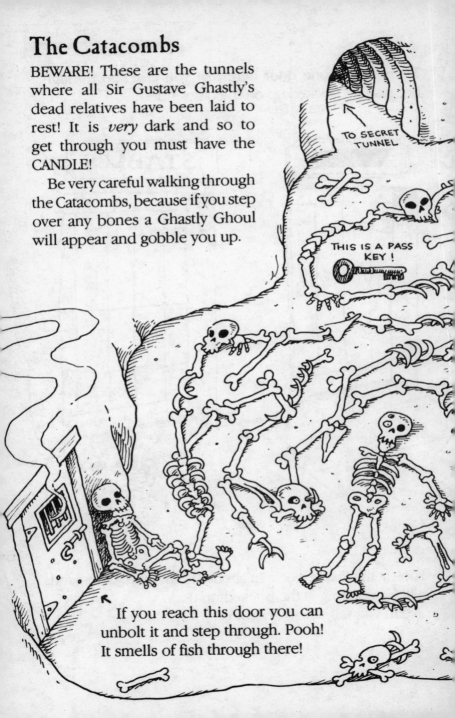

TO SECRET TUNNEL

THIS IS A PASS KEY !

If you reach this door you can unbolt it and step through. Pooh! It smells of fish through there!

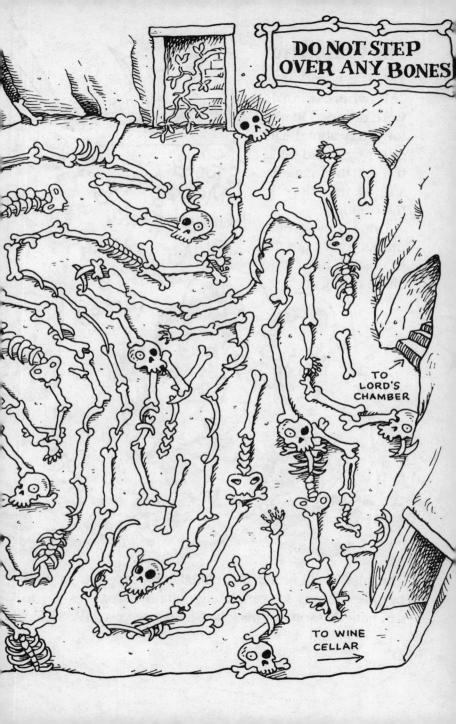

The Oubliette

This is a horrid, dark cell where people were dropped in and forgotten about! The only way in and out is through the strangely-shaped trap door in the ceiling.

Don't come in here unless you've got the ROPE to help you climb out again.

Stocky Cheeky Monkey Hanky Tricky Flaky Sticky Funky Turkey

The mad court jester, Ray Zallaf, was dropped in here because he was so completely unfunny. However, if you can help Ray sort out his jokes, he'll give you a PASS KEY!

Here are a list of his jokes. Can you put the answers in the spaces provided?

What kind of key is difficult?

— — = — — —

What kind of key hates Christmas?

= — — — — —

What kind of key is a hot toffee?

— — = — — —

What kind of key is a bit fat?

= — — — — —

What kind of key crumbles?

— — = — —

What kind of key likes groovy music?

= — — — —

What kind of key can you blow your nose on?

— = — — —

What kind of key lives in trees?

— — — = — —

What kind of key is a bit rude?

— — — = — —

(To help you Ray has written the answers on the wall, they're a bit mixed up!)

Before you go, there's a very important message about the PASS KEY Ray has given you . . . read down the double underlined letters.

The Lake

Right under the Castle is a massive lake. It's so dark and horrid that all the fish die and float to the top, which makes an awful stink!

Apart from dead fish, you'll see some objects are floating in the Lake . . . but which one should not be floating? Take it with you because it's MAGIC!

If you look up you'll see a hole in the rock ceiling right over the middle of the Lake.

At the edge of the water is a narrow ledge leading to a door. This is the only way out, but the door won't open unless you've first unbolted it from the other side!

The Bathroom

What are you staring at? Haven't you ever seen a spider in a bath before? This is Grimly the legendary Ghastlie Spydere of ye Castle. He is so ghastly, he bathes in acid.

Hanging over the washbasin is a MIRROR which you can take with you . . . if you can get to it!

In crossing from the door to the mirror, Grimly will only let you burst a maximum of three bubbles. Any more and he will grab you and dunk you in his acid bath!

The Lord's Chamber

This is the room where Sir Gustave used to sleep. Because he was so nastily fiendish, he was very careful to make himself as safe from his enemies as possible. That's why he had the main door nailed up.

The only way in and out of his room is the staircase to the Catacombs . . . unless you've found the four MAGIC NUMBERS in four other rooms in the Castle. Have you found them? If so, add all four numbers up and that will give you the MEGA MAGIC NUMBER!

Look at the three numbered doors. Two of them are trick doors which are just glued to the wall. However, you *can* open the one marked with the MEGA MAGIC NUMBER! You'll have to look through the book to see where it comes out, though . . .

The Gun Room

All of the guns in the Gun Room used to be attached to the wall by loops of string.

GUARDROOM

BULLET
SAVING
GUN

ELEPHANT
GUN

AIR
GUN

BLUNDERBUSS

STEREO
GUN

To GARRISON

The only one that works is still attached. Can you find it?

The Grey Bedroom

Nobody liked sleeping in the Grey Bedroom. It's one of the smallest, pokiest rooms in the Castle, and on Sunday mornings it was also very noisy! Can you work out why?

(It looks like somebody's been in and left a message, too!)

The Treasure Vault

What brains! What cunning! What downright utter and total brilliance!

Sir Gustave very carefully converted his own personal garderobe into this secret Treasure Vault.

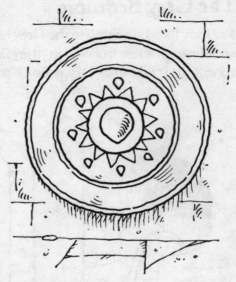

There's tons of treasure in here. That's why the door is made out of impregnable titanium.

Here's a list of all the treasure that Sir Gustave pinched, stole, nicked, borrowed without giving back, embezzled, purloined, plundered and was given for birthdays and Christmas presents:

DIAMOND BRACELET
PEARLS
RUBY EARRINGS
SAPPHIRE BROOCH
TIARA
GOLD COINS
SILVER TOOTHBRUSH
EMERALD TEAPOT
MARBLE CLOCK
CASH

All the treasures in the vault are hidden in this word grid. Words can read forwards and backwards and up and down, diagonally, *and* they can also read round corners!

(Somebody has already found "Diamond bracelet" for you.)

E	L	B	P	P	H	S
C	R	M	G	A	I	L
O	L	A	N	S	R	A
C	D	I	R	B	E	P
K	T	E	A	R	H	T
E	Y	E	M	O	U	O
A	B	D	N	O	S	O
P	U	R	A	C	H	T
O	C	A	I	L	E	R
T	H	S	T	V	O	G

Actually there is one of Sir Gustave's treasures that isn't here! Which one doesn't appear in the grid?

The Turkish Bedroom

Whoops . . . keep your head down! There are a lot of deadly snakes flying around in here on a magic carpet.

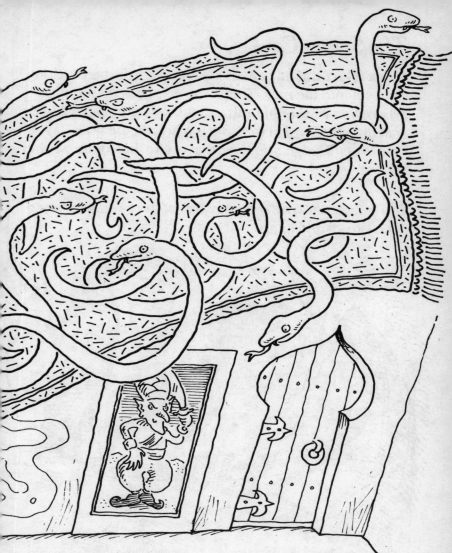

Look at the strange bottle on the table! It looks as though it might be helpful. If you want to know what's in the bottle, the pattern in the carpet tells you. You'll have to try to ignore the snakes!

The Secret Cave

At one end of this tiny cave beneath the Castle there's a long slide cut into the rock. There's no way back up the slide – it's been worn very smooth and is covered in green slime.

At the other end of the cave is a hole in the floor. If you look over the edge, you'll see that you're directly above the Lake.

You guessed it! The only way out of the cave is to take a deep breath and jump . . .

Before you go, you'll notice a little box. Look at the circle of letters on the wall above it.

Start with the letter "T" then move round the circle, writing down every fifth letter you come to. Maybe the box is worth taking with you!

— — — — — — — — — — — —

— — — — — — — — —

The Goblin Den

The only way in and out of the Goblin Den is through the hole in the ceiling!

Down here is where all the nastiest little sprites of the Castle lived. They had black fingernails and green teeth, but worst of all they had simply dreadful table manners. (That's because they were always goblin.)

OT ES HE WO OT EM SA RU 9E
GK FO AB LT VI RE OL KO NU
ED TR EH AT LB IE TN EH BO
ES VR TA RO Y

NI HT AE MR
UO YR OL KO
OF TR EH HS
EI DL IW HT
UO AT YN OC
WB BE S

UB TY EH EP AN EX ET
TA WO LE NA SD EW TE
IS TN EH UG RA RD OO M

The Goblins were quite clever and they made lots of helpful notes about the Castle. The trouble is that they are written in GOBLIN LANGUAGE! You'll have to find instructions on how to read Goblin language somewhere else.

The Pantry

There's all sorts of food in here, but it's all gone mouldy! See if you can tell what's on the mixed-up labels! (Remember, everything is MOULDY!)

The Bedroom Landing

Leading from the Bedroom Landing are some stairs and five funny doors. The floor is very dangerous!

When you go along the landing you must take very tiny soft steps . . . in fact you must only step from one floorboard to the next. The only safe floorboards are fastened down at both ends with big round nails.

TO THE
PORTRAIT
GALLERY

Whatever you do, don't step on the unsafe boards (and don't step on the holes, of course), or you'll plummet right through the floor and be stuck down there for *ever*.

(If you find a path to one of the funny-shaped doors, you'll have to look through the book to see which room the door opens into.)

The Well House

The Castle well isn't used any more. Sir Gustave threw so many enemies down it, it got blocked up!

Some of the old ropes for the well are still lying about. Sadly, they're a bit frayed in places, which makes them very dangerous, especially for climbing! They've also got a bit tangled up.

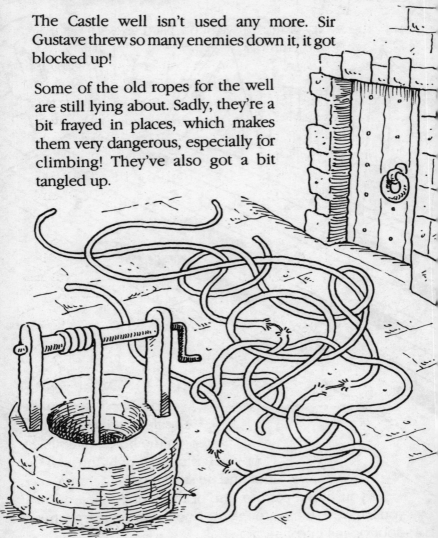

Can you find one ROPE that is safe enough to be useful?

The Aviary

Here's the Aviary where Sir Gustave used to keep his pet rooks, ravens and vultures.

The birds were so vicious that Sir Gustave built a set of eight bewitched scarecrows to guard them. These awesome effigies can suddenly come alive and attack anyone or anything that touches them!

Each of the evil scarecrows has a matching partner, but there is a ninth SCARECROW which is safe.

Can you tell which one it is? It might be useful.

The Chapel

The Chaplain is delighted that you've come to look round the Chapel, but first he insists that you help his good works by donating some GOLD COINS!

Once you've helped the Chaplain, you might notice the door round the corner.

If you colour in the dotted sections you will see a pattern on the door. The same pattern is repeated on the other side of the door . . . so look through the book to see where the door comes out!

The Billiard Room

The Billiard Room has a doorway leading to the Great Hall, but it also has an OBVIOUS PANEL. (An obvious panel is actually a secret panel which isn't very secret.)

As the obvious panel is a bit obvious, Sir Gustave played a very dirty trick. He booby-trapped it! If you open the panel without disarming the trap, then a 900 tonne weight covered in jagged spikes all dripping with poison will fall on you.

Look at the billiard table. All the balls are numbered. To disarm the booby trap you must knock in four different balls which together add up to forty-one points. Which four balls should you knock in?

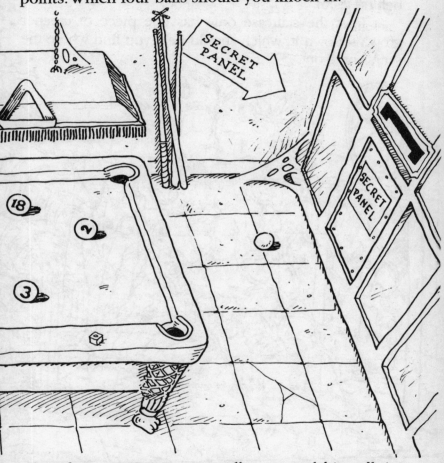

Don't forget, Sir Gustave was really mean and this really is a dirty trick!

The Conservatory

The Ghastly plant collection has gone a bit wild! The plants have covered most of the room and you can't see what's behind them.

At least the staircase only has one piece of creeper growing down it, which should help you find where the stairs come out.

There is a main door behind one of the plants, but it can only be unlocked from the other side. You can find out what the door is made from by solving this riddle:

My first is in night
  but never in day
My second is found in both
  laughter and play
My third is in apple
  and also in peach
my fourth is in sand,
  but not in a beach
my last is in scarlet
  but never in green
and my whole is quite
            solid,

  yet often
        unseen.

The Observatory

This is where Sir Gustave's astronomers used to work. The solid steel door has to be opened from the other side before you can use it!

On the table are some photographs taken through the telescope. Sir Gustave's astonomers used to have competitions.

They scored:

One point for a star ☆ Two points for a planet ☆ Three points for the moon.

Here are the photographs. Which one scored the highest points?

Incidentally, the highest score is one of the four MAGIC NUMBERS!

The Secret Tunnel

Pooh! The air is smelly in here! The door at the end of the tunnel leads to the Catacombs. But what's that noise?

A giant two-headed dog lives down here. Before you can pass through you'll need to feed him, and there's only one thing he likes eating (apart from people!).

To find out what you need to get, help the spider get to the fly. Can you find the path along the web which spells out a strange type of food?

When you've worked out what the food is, you'll have to get it before you pass the dog!

The Laundry

Oh dear! The Laundry washing machine has just exploded and fired socks everywhere. This means that, just like in any other laundry, a lot of socks have gone missing!

If you leave out the matching pairs, how many odd socks are there? It's worth holding your nose and counting them up because ... this is a MAGIC NUMBER!

The Guard Room

Some of the enterprising Guards have turned the Guard Room into the Ghastly Gifte Shoppe. Look at the super range of souvenirs! Luckily, you find a £10 note on the floor, but the Guards will not let you through until you've spent the whole £10 exactly.

You can't buy more than one of anything, and you can't take away anything you don't buy. What are you going to buy?

(By the way, once you've spent your £10, you can pass
through here as often as you like.)

The Clock Room

All of these clocks tell different times, but we do know that one of them is correct!

Of the others one is five hours fifty-five mins slow, one is four hours and fifteen mins fast, one is one hour thirty-five mins slow, and one is one hour and forty mins fast.

Which clock is correct?

There are only two clocks in the whole Castle that show the right time. The other one is just through this doorway!

The Flag Room

The Flag Room has flags all over the walls which match with the patterns on the floor. However, one pattern does not match with a flag, and is in fact a funny-shaped trap door! Can you spot it? Look through the book to see where it leads.

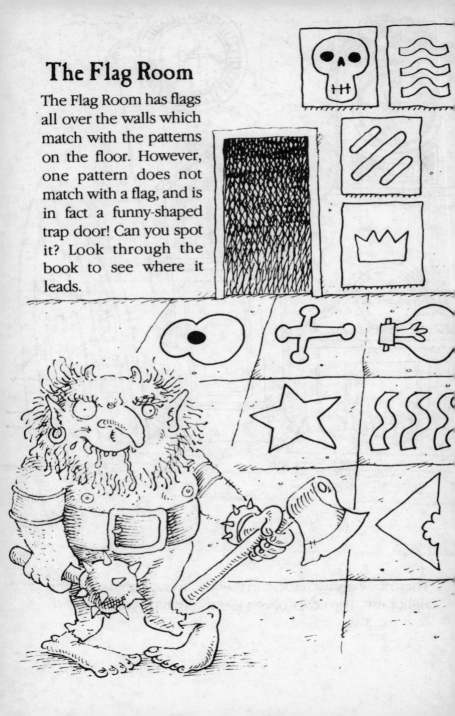

Before you open the trap door, you'll have to fight the Mad Troll. For this you'll need the MAGIC SWORD!

The Dining Room

Oh yuk! Look at the dirty plates! The table hasn't been cleared since Sir Gustave's last banquet here. Before you can bear to step through here, you'll need the INCENSE to improve the smell.

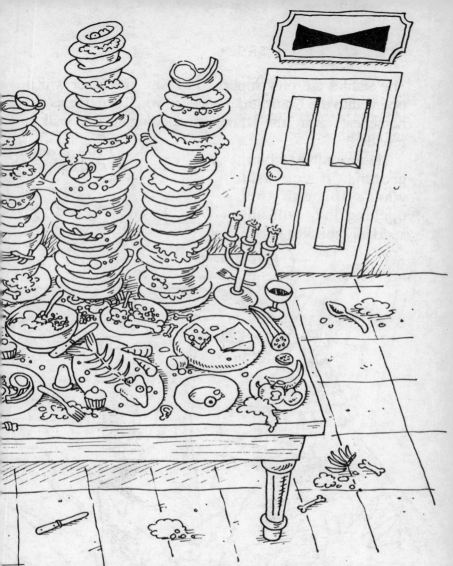

The dwarf wants you to feed his goat before he lets you through. The goat is a bit strange – it only eats food that begins with the letter C. Can you find six things to give him?

The Stables

The Stables are only supposed to have one door which opens into the Courtyard. However, you'll see that as the horse eats away the straw, an opening in the wall is revealed!

There are five Goblin grooms. If you ask what's through the opening they will all suddenly speak at once!

Actually, four of them are lying. So where does the opening go?

WARNING: It is unwise to go through the hole unless you have already unbolted the door in the Catacombs.

The Garrison

Sir Gustave had a lot of posh signs made to go round his Castle, but sadly the middle bits kept breaking and falling out. All the broken bits were brought in here to be mended by the off-duty soldiers.

GUN ROOM

CLOCK ROOM

DINING ROO

ARMOURY

CHAPEL

GARRISON

MARBLE PASSAGE

GAMES ROOM

BEDROOM LANDING

There are even two broken signs in here. Can you see which pieces should fit them and work out where the doors lead to?

WELL HOUSE

BATTLEMENTS

FLAG ROOM

CONSERVATORY

BATTLEMENTS

LABORATORY

KITCHEN

(By the way, all the other bits of signs will fit other places in the Castle!)

The Study

This is where Professor Wryte-Nuttah spent many long years trying to understand Goblin writing!

He finally discovered that all you do is swap round every pair of letters and then arrange the spaces to make words.

For instance, Goblin birthday cards have
AH PP BY RI HT AD Y written on them.

If you swap round the pairs of letters
you get:

HA PP YB IR TH DA Y (You can't swap
round the last letter because it's got
nothing to swap with!)

Then, if you change the spaces you get
HAPPY BIRTHDAY

First of all, try and decode this Goblin joke:

HW DY DI HT FE TA NG MO
SE TI NO TA AO SD OT LO?

EB AC SU TE EH ER AW NS MT SU
RH OO OM TN EH UM HS OR MO.

As you can see, Goblin jokes aren't all that funny. But now
you've got the hang of it, here's your first *important* Goblin
message to try and decode:

HT SE CE ER AT MR UO YR OD RO
EL DA TS TO EH UD GN OE N

By the way, look out for other Goblin messages left all
round the Castle!

The Laboratory

There are two ways in and out of the Laboratory: some stairs going up to the Turret, and a solid steel door which leads to the Observatory.

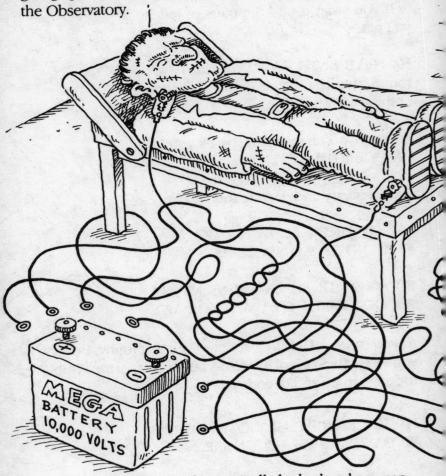

The door is electronically locked and you can only open it by connecting the two door wires to the two battery terminals.

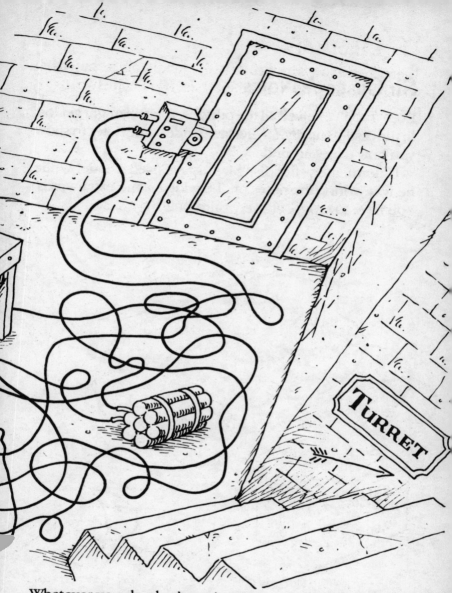

Whatever you do, don't get it wrong – you might wake up the monster, or explode the dynamite.

Sir Gustave's Notes

Even if you've solved all the puzzles, you still might get lost in the castle! Luckily, Sir Gustave made some notes to show you how to get around.

Unfortunately, fiendish Sir Gustave used a code! While he was writing the notes out he added some extra words. You have to cross out every third one.

NOTES

From Gatehouse drawbridge go into Garrison Courtyard then Armoury to Lower Battlements Battlements, through Stables Guardroom, Gun Flag Room, Garrison Stables and to Kitchen Armoury (get CANDLE HACKSAW) Return go to Battlements Pantry. Cut open stairs gate.

Go return through Pink Courtyard Bedroom to Turret Bedroom Landing. Return from there Bedroom you can get get to GOLD Nursery (and Conservatory down into Oubliette Goblin Den), to Bathroom (get KEY MIRROR), Turkish Grey Bedroom (get out INCENSE), Portrait Landing Gallery.

From Bathroom Portrait Gallery Turkish to Clock Billiard Room (and Conservatory into Study Library get GOBLIN SWORD CODE) through Flag Games Room and to Aviary Observatory (get SCARECROW ROPE).

Return to Battlements Portrait Gallery, and through Hall stairs to Library (get look on CLOCK the table). Then return to Armoury Portrait Gallery stairs then retrace Hall right back up to Battlements. Go enter door Catacombs to Laundry Dungeon then Kitchen Passage (get the SWORD CANDLE) to Lake Pantry (get KEY MOULDY SAUSAGES) back through Wine Salt Cellar to Cave Catacombs to Chapel Lord's Chamber.

Return back via Lake Catacombs to Belfry Kitchen. To Chapel Dining Room, Dungeon, Marble Passage, portcullis Hall to Gatehouse Billiard Room. Continue retrace via Hall Kitchen to Chapel Battlements. Through Belfry Turret to Aviary Laboratory and Conservatory on to Library Observatory. Return HACKSAW to Battlements, Armoury continue through Courtyard to

Armoury, Stables then through
hole secret door slide to Dungeon,
Cave, Secret Passage Vault,
Catacombs and Cellar unbolt door go
to Lake.
Swim go right across back to ledge
Courtyard, into Catacombs Well House
Dungeon (get ROPE BLUNDERBUSS).
Then from Armoury Courtyard into
Guardroom Stables, slide climb down
into Wine Cave get SCARECROW GOLD.
Drop dive into Lake Oubliette (get
SWORD KEY), back through Garrison
Catacombs again get to Garrison
INCENSE. Go to Clock Flag Room
Study, and down unlock through trap
glass door to conservatory Oubliette.
Go through right back doorway
via Battlements Kitchen and Portrait
Bedroom Gallery to Vault Chapel,
Through Nursery to Belfry window
through wall door into Grey Pink
Bedroom. Go return back to from
Lord's Chamber Lake and into Catacombs
Secret Treasure Passage Vault. Where
haven't haven't you you managed to
reached go?

Special Phantom-finder Pages

These pages are for you to keep track of the rooms you've visited, and any useful items you've found in them.

Page	Tick	Room	What You've Found!
8	☐	Gate House	
10	☐	Dungeon	
12	☐	Marble Passage	
14	☐	Great Hall	
16	☐	Kitchen	
18	☐	Belfry	
20	☐	Nursery	
22	☐	Games Room	
24	☐	Library	
26	☐	Turret	
28	☐	Battlements	
30	☐	Portrait Gallery	
32	☐	Armoury	
34	☐	Wine Cellar	
36	☐	Pink Bedroom	
38	☐	Courtyard	
40	☐	Catacombs	
42	☐	Oubliette	

HAVE YOU BEEN
TO ALL THE ROOMS
IN THE CASTLE?

If you got all the puzzles right and didn't cheat, you'll find there was just one room you couldn't possibly get into. This is where the Phantom is trapped!

Did you find the special instructions for actually seeing the Phantom? If not, you'd better look until you do find them!

So, if you DARE . . . turn back the pages to find the haunted room and follow the special instructions. Get your evilest laugh ready, because maybe, just maybe . . .

You will see the Phantom!